Street by Street

WAKEF|

CASTLEFORD

KNOTTINGLEY, NORMANTON, PONTEFRACT

Ackworth Moor Top, Crofton, East Ardsley, Featherstone, Fitzwilliam, Hemsworth, Horbury, Ossett, South Elmsall, South Kirkby, Walton

1st edition September 2002

© Automobile Association Developments Limited 2002

Ordnance Survey® This product includes map data licensed from Ordnance Survey® with the permission of the Controller of Her Majesty's Stationery Office. © Crown copyright 2002. All rights reserved. Licence No: 399221.

Published by AA Publishing (a trading name of Automobile Association Developments Limited, whose registered office is Millstream, Maidenhead Road, Windsor, Berkshire SL4 5GD. Registered number 1878835).

The Post Office is a registered trademark of Post Office Ltd. in the UK and other countries.

Schools address data provided by Education Direct.

One-way street data provided by:

Tele Atlas   © Tele Atlas N.V.

Mapping produced by the Cartographic Department of The Automobile Association. A01100

A CIP Catalogue record for this book is available from the British Library.

Printed by GRAFIASA S.A., Porto, Portugal

The contents of this atlas are believed to be correct at the time of the latest revision. However, the publishers cannot be held responsible for loss occasioned to any person acting or refraining from action as a result of any material in this atlas, nor for any errors, omissions or changes in such material. This does not affect your statutory rights. The publishers would welcome information to correct any errors or omissions and to keep this atlas up to date. Please write to Publishing, The Automobile Association, Fanum House (FH17), Basing View, Basingstoke, Hampshire, RG21 4EA.

Ref: ML206

ii

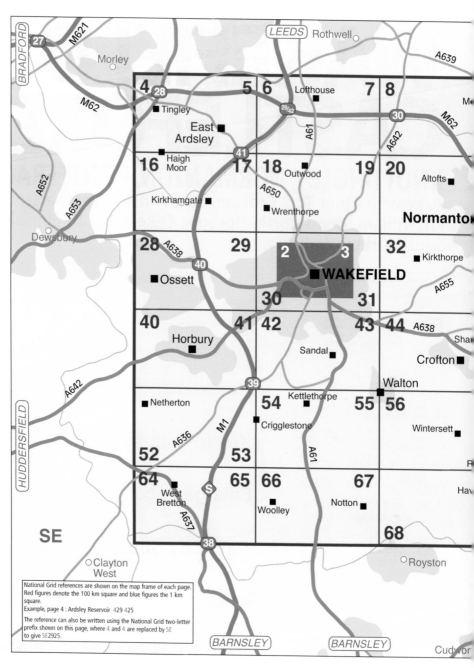

National Grid references are shown on the map frame of each page.
Red figures denote the 100 km square and blue figures the 1 km
square.
Example, page 4 : Ardsley Reservoir 429 425
The reference can also be written using the National Grid two-letter
prefix shown on this page, where 4 and 4 are replaced by SE
to give SE2925.

Enlarged scale pages   **1:10,000**   6.3 inches to 1 mile

0 — 1/4 — miles — 1/2
0 — 1/4 — 1/2 — kilometres — 3/4 — 1

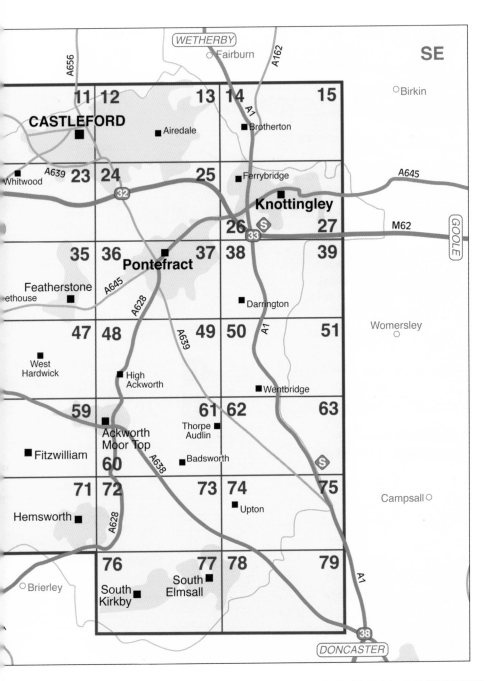

A656

WETHERBY
○ Fairburn

A162

SE

○ Birkin

| 11 | 12 | | 13 | 14 | | 15 |

CASTLEFORD

A1

■ Airedale

■ Brotherton

| 23 | 24 | | 25 |

A639

Whitwood ■

32

Ferrybridge ■

A645

Knottingley

| 26 | 27 |

S

33

M62

GOOLE

| 35 | 36 | 37 | 38 | | 39 |

Pontefract

Featherstone

A645

ethouse ■

A628

Darrington ■

| 47 | 48 | 49 | 50 | | 51 |

A639

A1

Womersley
○

West
Hardwick ■

High ■
Ackworth

Wentbridge ■

| 59 | 61 | 62 | | 63 |

Ackworth ■
Moor Top

Thorpe ■
Audlin

Fitzwilliam ■

A638

| 60 |

Badsworth ■

S

| 71 | 72 | 73 | 74 | | 75 |

Hemsworth ■

A628

Upton ■

Campsall ○

| 76 | 77 | 78 | | 79 |

South ■
Kirkby

South ■
Elmsall

A1

○ Brierley

38

DONCASTER

4.2 inches to 1 mile   **Scale of main map pages** **1:15,000**

| 0 | 1/4 | miles | 1/2 | 3/4 | 1 |

| 0 | 1/4 | 1/2 | kilometres 3/4 | 1 | 1 1/4 | 1 1/2 |

Symbol	Description	Symbol	Description
Junction 9	Motorway & junction	⊖	Underground station
Services	Motorway service area	⊖	Light railway & station
	Primary road single/dual carriageway	++++++++	Preserved private railway
Services	Primary road service area	LC	Level crossing
	A road single/dual carriageway	•—•—•—•	Tramway
	B road single/dual carriageway	----------	Ferry route
	Other road single/dual carriageway	....	Airport runway
	Minor/private road, access may be restricted	— · — · — · —	County, administrative boundary
← ←	One-way street	ꝟꝟꝟꝟꝟꝟꝟ	Mounds
	Pedestrian area	**17**	Page continuation 1:15,000
============	Track or footpath	**3**	Page continuation to enlarged scale 1:10,000
▮▮▮▮▮▮▮▮ ▮▮▮▮▮▮▮▮	Road under construction		River/canal, lake, pier
⊦ — — — ⊣	Road tunnel		Aqueduct, lock, weir
AA	AA Service Centre	465 ▲ Winter Hill	Peak (with height in metres)
P	Parking		Beach
P+🚌	Park & Ride		Woodland
🚌	Bus/coach station		Park
	Railway & main railway station	✝	Cemetery
	Railway & minor railway station		Built-up area

Featured building		Abbey, cathedral or priory	
City wall		Castle	
Hospital with 24-hour A&E department		Historic house or building	
Post Office		National Trust property	
Public library		Museum or art gallery	
Tourist Information Centre		Roman antiquity	
Petrol station Major suppliers only		Ancient site, battlefield or monument	
Church/chapel		Industrial interest	
Public toilets		Garden	
Toilet with disabled facilities		Arboretum	
Public house AA recommended		Farm or animal centre	
Restaurant AA inspected		Zoological or wildlife collection	
Theatre or performing arts centre		Bird collection	
Cinema		Nature reserve	
Golf course		Visitor or heritage centre	
Camping AA inspected		Country park	
Caravan Site AA inspected		Cave	
Camping & caravan site AA inspected		Windmill	
Theme park		Distillery, brewery or vineyard	

Wakehurst Place NT

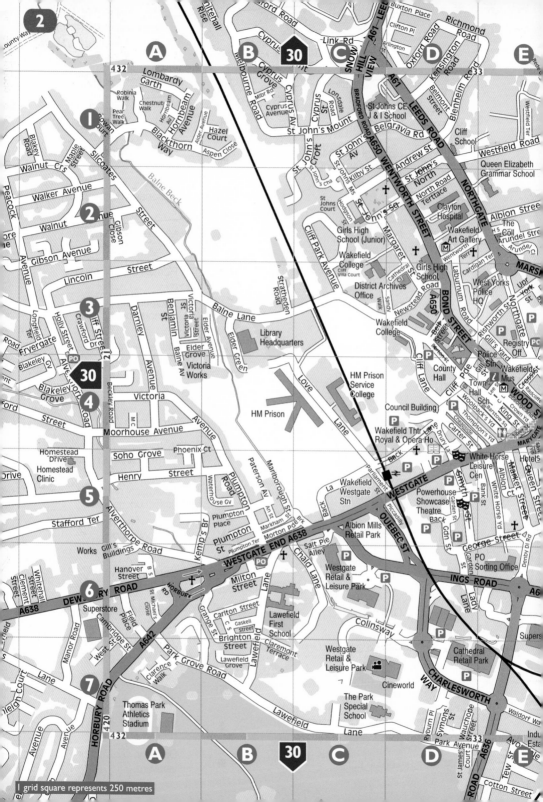

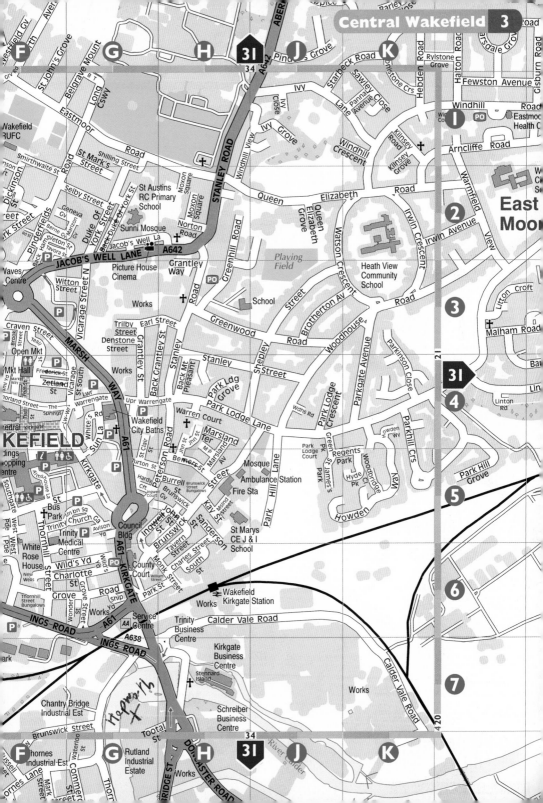

I grid square represents 500 metres

Main Street

Little
Carr Lane

New Rd

Unity
St

Chapel
St

Town Street

E

Carlton

F

G

H

Pit Field Road

34

35

27

Sanderson Lane

I

Pennington L

**Royds
Green**

Carlton
Cricket Club

Carlton Northfield
AFC

Lane

Ouzlewell
Green

Dungeon
Lane Farm

Dungeon Lane

2

LANE **B6135**

Crnmoor Crs

Green Bk

The
Fields

Beechcroft

**Ouzlewell
Green**

26

Lofthouse

M62

Coney

Lee Moor Lane

Lee Beck Grove

B6135

CASTLE

GATE

Sanderson Lane

3

8

**Lee
Moor**

Common Road

Fenton Road

4

425

Moorhot

Moorho

West Ha
Special

ouse

Stanley Sports
& Social Club

Moor Road

Moor
Gv

Moor Av

Lee Moor Rd

Rogers Ct

P M6

St Peter's Crs

Holmfield Cha

Nettleton St

Barkl

PO

ABERFORD ROAD

5

Lofthousegate
J & I School

Millcroft

Millcroft Cl

Mill Rl

Canal Lane

Keats Grove

Havon Gv

Stannmoor Dr

Byron Gv

Chaucer Ct

Longfellow

Milton Cw

The Chase

A602

Trans Pennine Trail

al Lane

Langdale

Woolford W

34

Lake Lock Drive

35

Mount Road

Lake Lock

The
thorns

Baker

Gainsborough Way

E

F

Samuel
St

Hargreaves Av

19

useway

Chapel St

Stanley
St P
J&I ol

Stanley
Health
Centre

G

Church Road

Lake Lock Gv

Cemetery

Lake
Yard

H

Road

River

Michael Lane

Meadowcroft Rd

Rae Ct

Newlands Dr

Newlands

Noon Cl

Stonecrof

Broadm

Whisperw

Ravenwood

Brockenwood Rd

Lake

Beaumo

Marshall St

Intake

PO

Langd

Arrahe

Rd

8

A　B　C　D

436　37

Royds Green 1

Royds School

Sanderson Lane

Pennington Lane

WAKEFIELD ROAD

A642

Sugar Hill Close

Wordsworth Dr

Ilton Drive

Clumpcliffe

Leeds Country Way

Moss Carr

Leeds Country Way

2

26

Junction 30

M62

GATE

3 Sanderson Lane

7

B6135 NEWMARKET LANE

Met Lan

4

425

Moorhouse Grove

Moorhouse Av

Men Cl
M Ter
Scarth Ter
Ch Pl

Trans Pennine Trail

Bottom Boat

West Hall Special School

Mdwfld Pl

St Peter's Crs

Holmfield Cha

Nettleton St

Barker St

PO

Bottom Boat Road

5

ABERFO ROAD

A642

The ase

Old Canal

Trans Pennine Trail

Kings

Lake Yard

River Calder

A　B　**20**　C　D

436　37

Navigation

1 grid square represents 500 metres

Wood Row

E F G H

Methley Park Hospital

Woodrow Crs

Station Rd

Wood Row

The Hollings

LEEDS ROAD

Mulberry Cft

Little Church La

Church Lane

CHC VHS

T Orchards

Methley Infant School

Methley

Rothwell Methley CP Infant School

I

CHURCH SIDE

2

BARNSDALE ROAD

Park Lane

WATERGATE

Burnleys VW

Green Row

Burnleys Dr

Burnleys Court

PGC

PnGE

Pinders Gn

Pinders Gn

Hazel Rd

Dr Embleton Rd

ungate

Lane

ungate

B6135

Scholey Hill

Me Ju

3

10

Trans Pennine Trail

Leeds Wakefield

4

425

5

Express Way

Tuscany Way

Express Way

Tuscany WY

Tuscany Way

Express Way

Altoft

Altof

Lower Altofts

Lock Lane

38

21

Pope Street

39

E F G H

holes

Fernley Hill

Edward St

Pearson St

Express Way

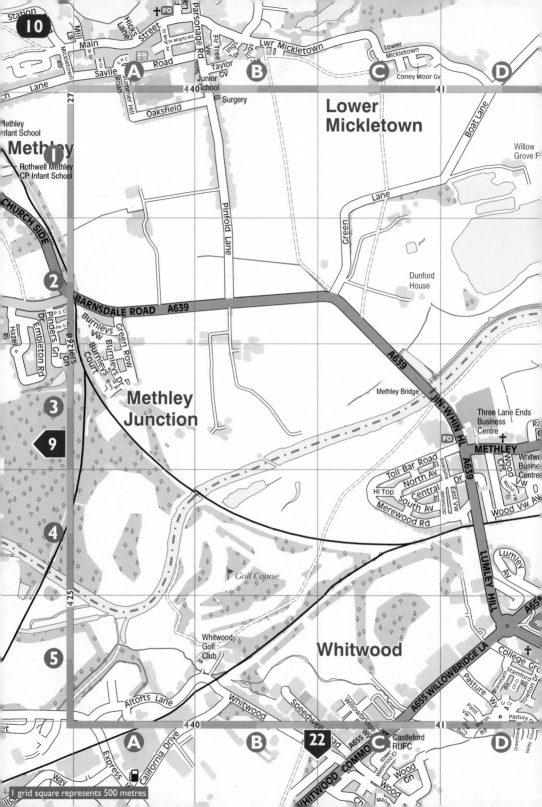

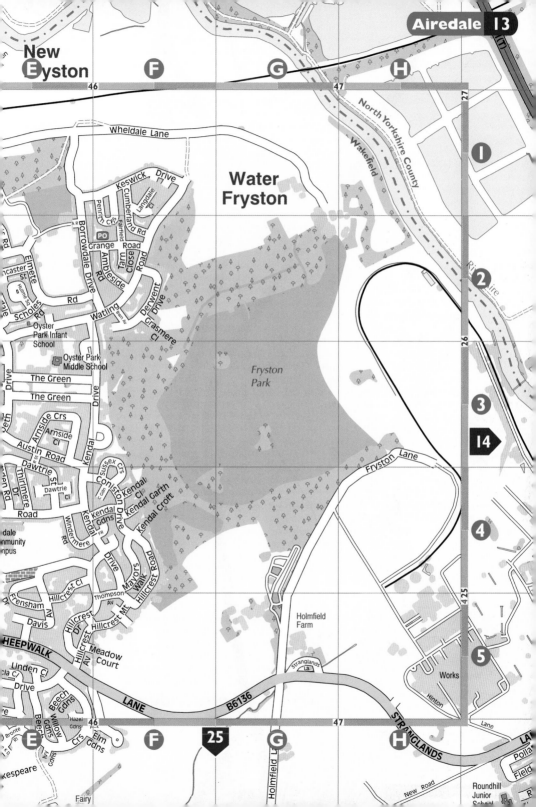

E   F   G   H

50   51

27

I

2

3

4

5

26

4 25

Byram Farm

Byram Park Road

Road

Sutton   Lane

Sutton Lane

Tippaty Lane

Sutton

Smeathalls
Farm

La

River

Birk

West Ings
Crescent

West Ings
Mews

West Ings
Lane

West Ings
Way

Croftlands   Aire St

St

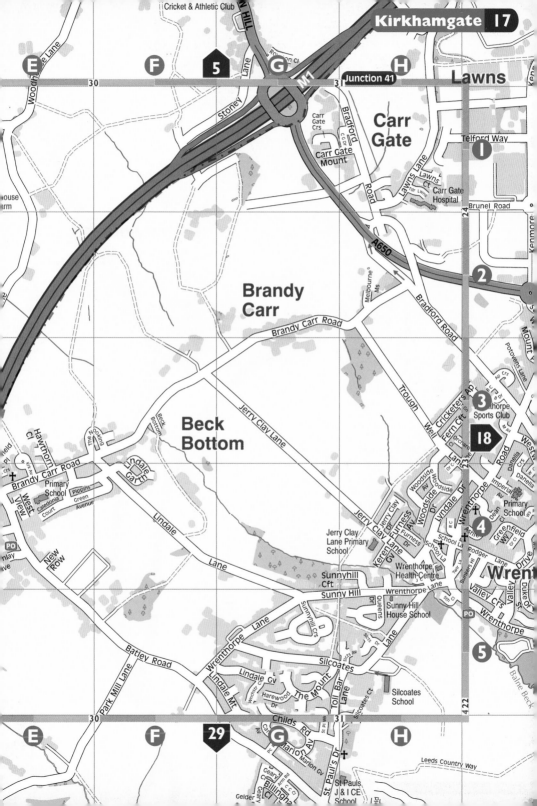

Cricket & Athletic Club

E F **5** G **M1** **Junction 41** H **Lawns**

30 3

Woodhouse Lane

Stoney Lane

Rougtton Cl

Bradford

Carr Gate

Carr Gate Crs

Carr Gate Mount

Lawns Ct

Lawns Lane

Lawns Tdr

Carr Gate Hospital

Telford Way **I**

Brunel Road

24

Road

A650

Melbourne Ms

2

Brandford Road

Brandy Carr

Brandy Carr Road

Trough Well

Cricketers Ap

Fern Cft

Potovens Lane

Ad Crs

Mount

3

Wrenthorpe Sports Club

18

Orchard

West

Danella Ct

Danella

Beck Bottom

Beck Bottom

Jerry Clay Lane

Lane

Woodside Av

Woodside Dr

Woodside

Lyndale Dr

Wrenthorpe Road

Dean

Imperial Av

Primary School

4

Greenfield Wy

Hawthorn Cl

The Nooking

Brandy Carr Road

Lindale Garth

West View

Primary School

Caledonia Court

Pippins Green Avenue

Lindale

Lane

Jerry Clay Lane

Jerry Clay Lane

Furness Av

Furness Dr

Kerenza Gv

School La

RC

Asholt

Dean

Rodger Lane

Valley Crs

Duke of

Wrent

New Row

Finlay Ave

PO

Jerry Clay Lane Primary School

Sunnyhill Cft

Wrenthorpe Health Centre

Wrenthorpe Lane

Blunkers Hl

Twrt La

PO

Valley Crs

5

Wrenthorpe

Balne Beck

Lindale Lane

Sunnyhill Crs

Sunny Hill

Queens

Lane

Sunny Hill House School

Batley Road

Park Mill Lane

30 31

Wrenthorpe Lane

Silcoates

Lindale Gv

The Mount

Lane

Toll Bar Lane

Silcoates Ct

Silcoates School

Lindale Mt

Webster Cft

Harewood Dr

Childs Rd

St Pl

Marion Gv

St Pauls Dr

E F **29** G H

30 31

Geary Cft

Billingham Cl

Marion Av

Gelder

St Pauls J & I CE School

Leeds Country Way

422

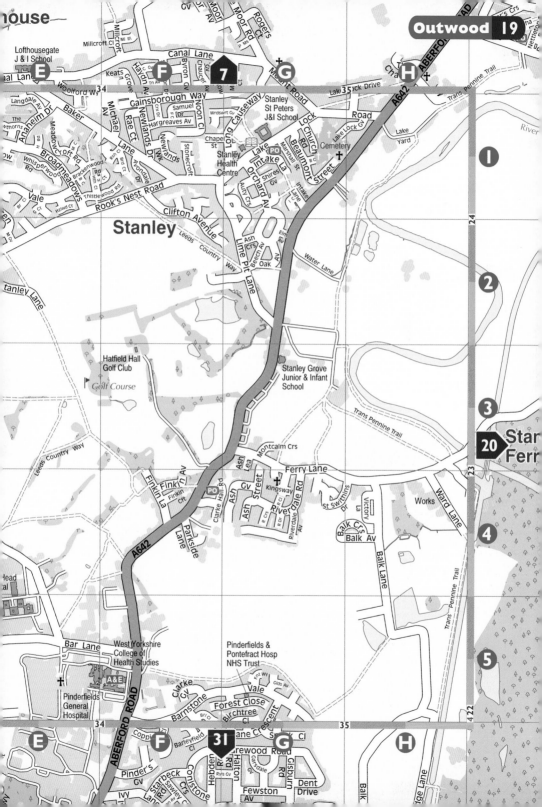

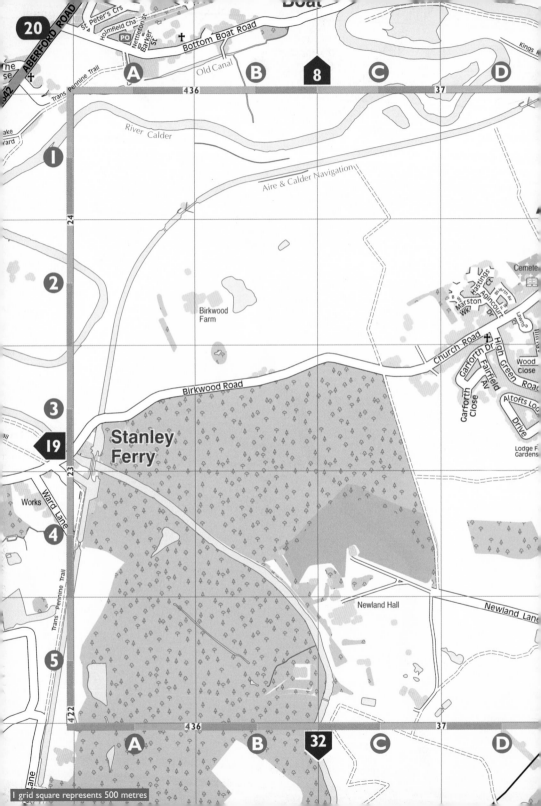

20

ABERFORD ROAD

St Peter's Crs
Holmfield Cha
Nettleton St
Barker St
PO

† Bottom Boat Road

Boat

Old Canal

Trans Pennine Trail

Kings

A **B** **8** **C** **D**

436 37

River Calder

I

24

Aire & Calder Navigation

2

Birkwood Farm

Cemete

Hastings
Agincourt
Marston
WK7
Marston

Church Road †

Garforth Dr
Garforth Close

High Green Road
FairField Av
Wood Close

Lawns

Altofts Lo

Birkwood Road

3

19

Stanley Ferry

23

Works

Ward Lane

4

Trans Pennine Trail

Lodge F
Gardens

DRIVE

Newland Hall

Newland Lane

5

422

436 37

A **B** **32** **C** **D**

Lane

1 grid square represents 500 metres

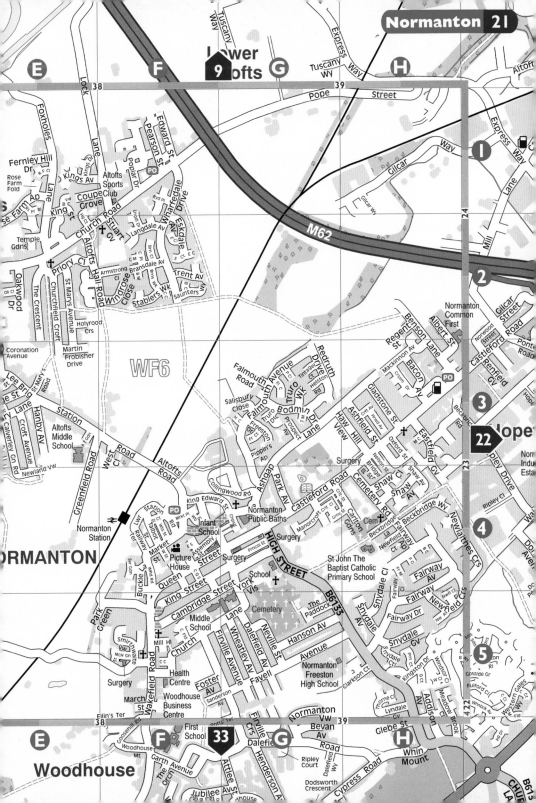

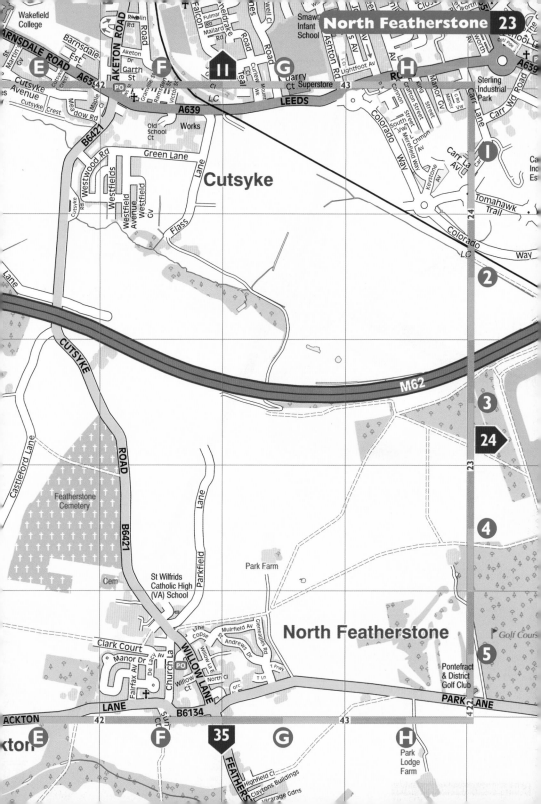

SHEEPWALK

E Meadow Court F 13 B6136 G H

Strglands La

Works

Hinton

LANE 46 47 STRANGLANDS La

Linden Ci

Acacia C

Drive

Beech Gdns

Willow Gdns

Hazel Gdns

Elm Gdns

Beech RI

Bronte RI

Shakespeare Rs

Fairy Hill

Holmfield Lane

New Road

Poli Field

I dhill Junior School

Cemetery

Wordsworth D

Hampden C

M62

24

2 Bronte Av

Orchard Head Drive

Orchard Head Primary School

Darkfield

Holmfield Lane

Holmfield

Holmfield Close

The Chestnuts

Askam Wyson Av

A Avenue

Ashdene Gv

Pontefract Road

Highfield

Highfield Av

Limetrees

3

New own

Sandhill

Abbey Gdns

Waterfall Fold

Orchard Head Lane

St Pauls C Ms

Ashworth Rd

Providence

Hinton

Banbury

St L Ha Ct

Orchrd

Mill Lane

Queensway

Road

Dulverton

Dulverton Rd

Dulverton

Manor Pk

Stumpcross

Stumpcross Wy

Sowgate La

3

26

illowdene La

St Ives Cl

Sandhill Ri

B Fall

Midgley Ri

Caxton Gdns

Chatsworth Av

Nevison Av

Wy

Highland Av

Dandy Ml

KNOTTINGLEY

23

ROAD

Nestfield Cl

Cavendish Av

The Ctyd

Harvest

Willow Bank

Elm Cl

Hazel Gv

Dandy Ml

Wy

Dandy Ml Av

Dn M Cft

Bexhill Close

Knottingley Rd

4

Longbull Hill

Lady Bronte Ct

Balk La

Monkhill La

Keats Cl

Tennyson

Kipling

Mt Coleridge

Wilsort Rd

Wntswrth Rd

Works

Ferrybridge

New Hall

Water La

422

Monkhill Av

Monkhill Drive

Pontefract Monkhill Station

Works

BONDGATE

Bond St

Box Lane

A645

BONDGATE

Cobblers Gdns

Stella Gdns

Cobblers La

Western Drive

Cobbler's Av

5

Monkhill

Black Wk

Mill Dam

Fox Ter

Atkinson La

Northfield

Springfield Av

Fieldmead

Scwth

Holy Family & St Michaels RC Primary School

Greavefield

Denwell Ter

St Giles CE VA Primary School

B Baileygate

Pontefract Castle

Castle Garth

S BAILEYGATE

Baileygate Infant Sch

Bondgate Industrial Est

Baileygate Industrial Est

Prall Cl

Fieldmead Cl

Cobblers Lane Junior & t School

Back Northgate

Micklegate

All Saints Industrial Est

Waterngate

Midland Rd

Eastfield Drive

Baghill La

Hallhead

Harefield Road

PO

Clinic

Sch

Pool

P.O. Sorting Office

Co Court

Station La

P

P

Baghill Station

E HGATE F De Lacy Ter Olivers Mt Fairfax R 37 G Baghill La H

Hillside Mt

Firnwell Crescent

South Vw Gdns

Willow

Eastbourne

Eastfield La

Pontefract General Infirmary

A&E

Harew

Worde

Wide

Fla

NEW ROAD 46 47

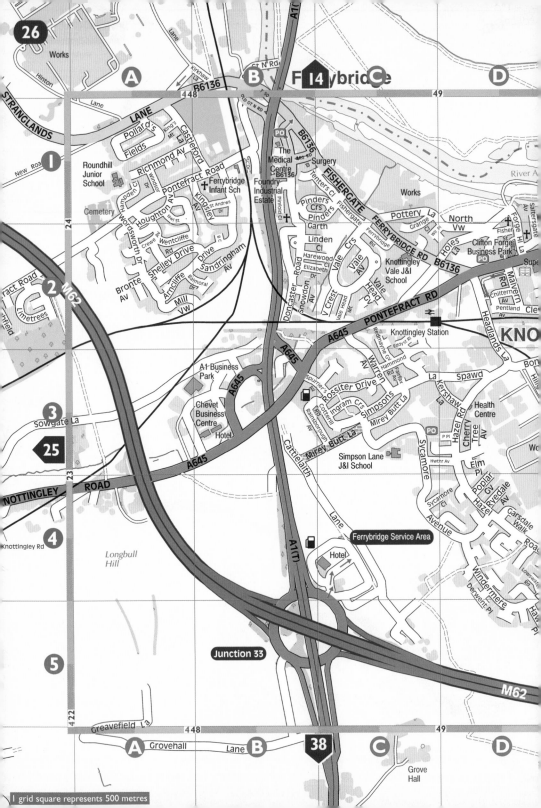

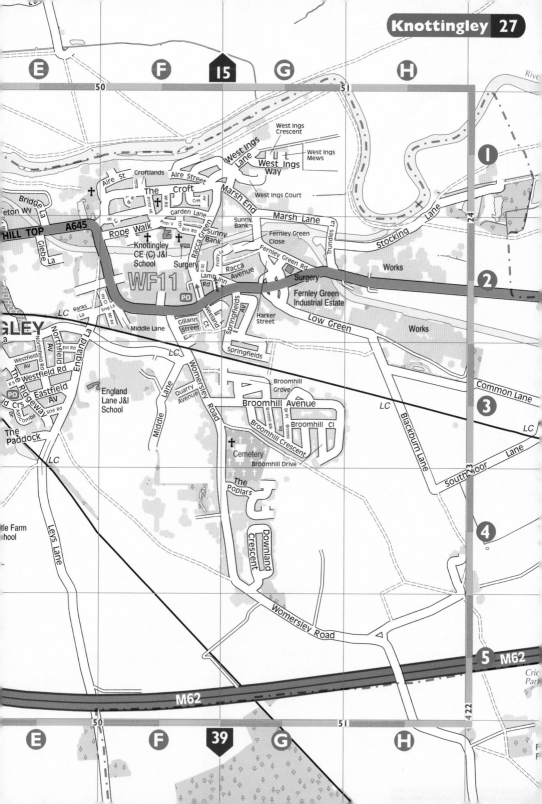

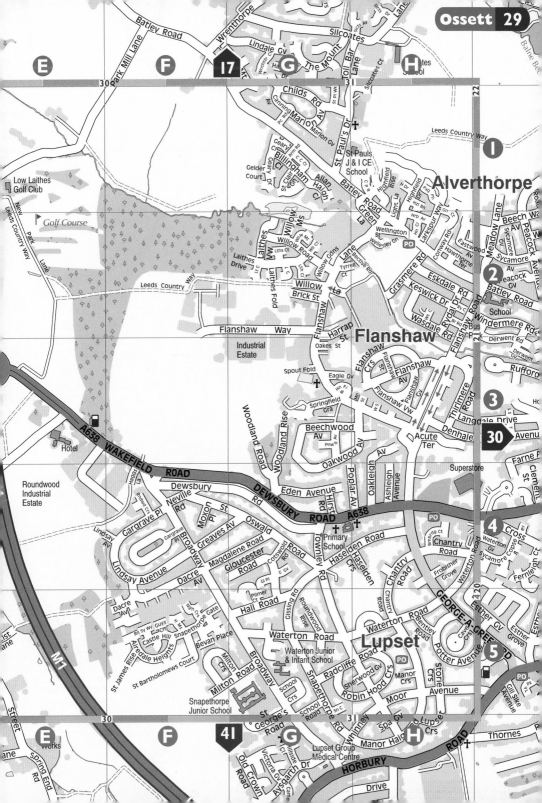

Batley Road

Wrenthorpe

Silcoates Lane

E

F

17

G

The Mount

Toll Bar Lane

Silcoates Ct

H

306 Park Mill Lane

31

22

Lindale Gv

Childs Rd

I

Leeds Country Way

Marion St

St Clair Rd

Marion Gv

Allan Haigh Cl

Batley Road Green La

St-Pauls J & I CE School

Highfield Rise

Alverthorpe

Billingham Rd

Gelder Court

Geary Dr

Light La

Highfield

Beech Wa

Meadow Lane

Sycamore Av

Low Laithes Golf Club

Willow Ms

Larkspur Way

Conway Rd

Eastwood

2

Peacock Gv

Sycamore Av

Golf Course

Laithes

Willow Road

Wellington St

Wellesley Gn

PO

Hawthorne

Batley Road

Windermere Rd

New Leeds Country Way

Park Lane

Laithes Drive

Laithes Fold

Lths Ct

Willow Gdns

Bective Rd

Grasmere Rd

Eskdale Rd

Keswick Dr

School

Bus

Leeds Country Way

Willow Brick St

Lane

Tyrrell St

Ct

Wasdale Rd

Rydal

Derwent Rd

Flanshaw Way

Flanshaw Lane

Harrap St

Oakes St

Flanshaw

Derwent Gv

Ruffora

Industrial Estate

Spout Fold

Eagle Gv

Flanshaw Crs

Flanshaw St

Flanshaw Av

Flanshaw Gv

Thirlmere

3

Woodland Road

Springfield Gra

Flanshaw Vw

Langdale Drive

Denhale

Avenu

Woodland Rise

Beechwood Av

Oakwood Av

Acute Ter

30

A638 WAKEFIELD ROAD

Hotel

Hagg La

Dewsbury Rd

Eden Avenue

Poplar Av

Oakleigh Av

Ashleigh Avenue

Superstore

Farne St

Clement St

Roundwood Industrial Estate

Gargrave Pl

Neville Rd

Moxon St

Greaves Av

Oswald Road

Townley Rd

Hirst Rd

DEWSBURY ROAD A638

Primary School

PO

Chantry Road

Frobisher Grove

Waterton Gv

Sycamore Cl

4

Cross

Lindsay Av

Cargrave Pl

Broadway

Magdalene Road

Gloucester Road

Haselden Road

Haselden Rd

Chantry Road

Waterton Road

Bentley Road

George-A-Cref Rd

Esther Gv

Esther Grove

Fernleigh

M1

Dacre Av

Hall Road

Gissing Rd

Cotswold Rd

Roundwood Rise

Waterton Road

Robin Hood Crs

Sherwood Gv

Manor Crs

Porter Avenue

5

Dacre Av

Lindsay Avenue

Bevan Place

Waterton Junior & Infant School

Lupset

PO

Moor Avenue

Gill Sike Av

St James Ri

Airedale Heights

Castle Hill

Snapethorpe Gate

St Bartholomews Court

Milton Road

Broadway

School Crs

Snapethorpe Road

Whinney Moor La

Spa Gv

Lupset Crs

Thornes

St James St

Snapethorpe Junior School

St George's Gv

E

F

41

G

Lupset Group Medical Centre

H

HORBURY ROAD

30

Old Crown Road

Aysgarth Dr

Hillside Gv

Victoria Gv

Camec

31

Manor Haig

LUPSET ROAD

Spring End Rd

Works

Drive

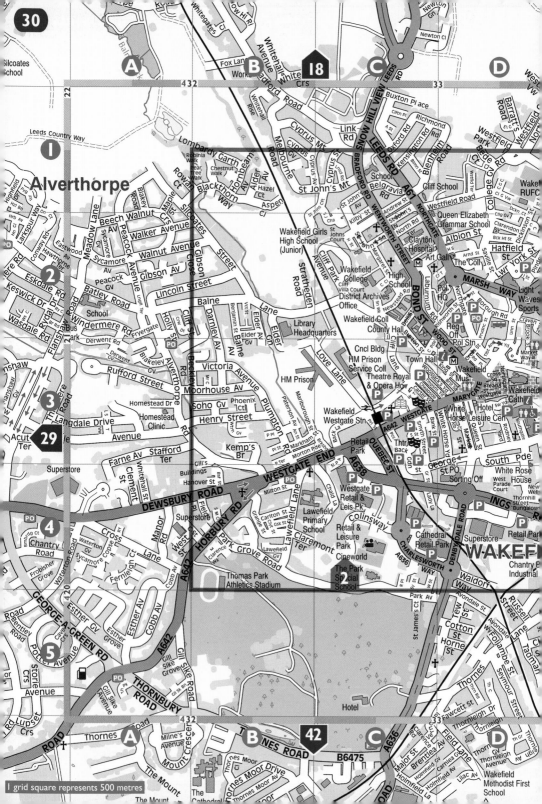

1 grid square represents 500 metres

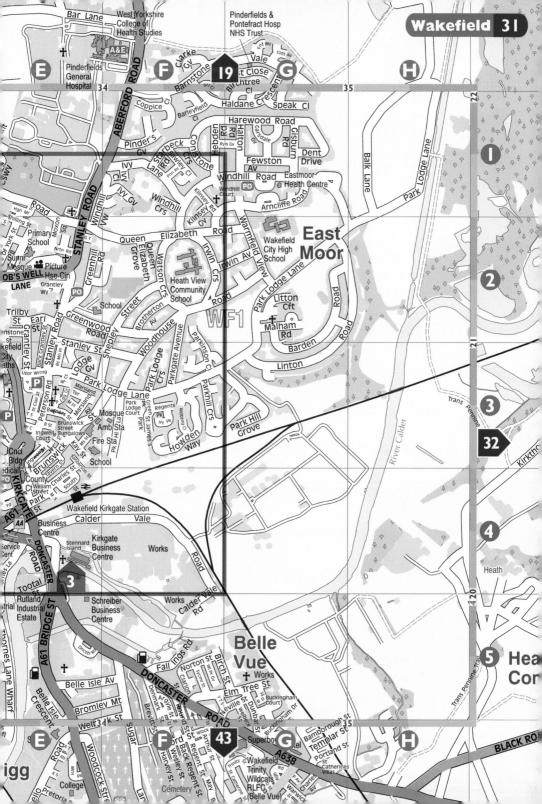

32

A   436   B   **20**   C   37   D

1

Park Lodge Lane

22

LC   **Goosehill**

2

21   Willow Lane   Gooseheill Lane

Church Avenue   Warmfield

Woodland Avenue   Park Av   **PO**   Croft Head

Half Moon Lane   ✝   Freston Drive   Freston Av

Kirkthorpe   **Warmfield**

3

Pennine Trail

Kirkthorpe Lane

31

Red

4

A655

Heath

A 20

Trans Pennine Trail

5

Heath Common

Hell Lane

A655

BLACK ROAD   A   436   B   **44**   C   37   D

A655

Burcroft Farm

I grid square represents 500 metres

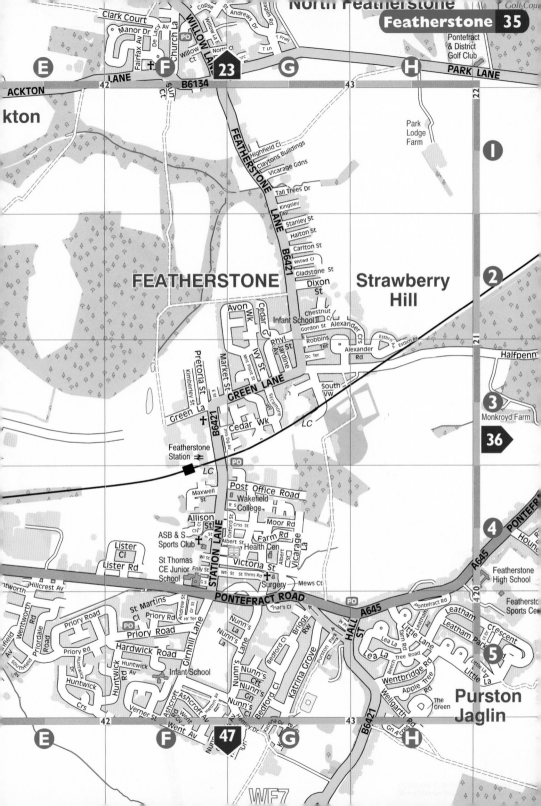

E   F   **M62** **27**   G   H

50   51   22

I

Leys

Stubbs Lane   LC

North Yorkshire County

Wakefield

2

21

3

Leys Road

Wake
Wood

4

Scrombeck
Farm

420

Bank Wood Road

North Lodge Lane

5

Works

50   51

E   F   **51**   G   H

Stapleton Park Farm

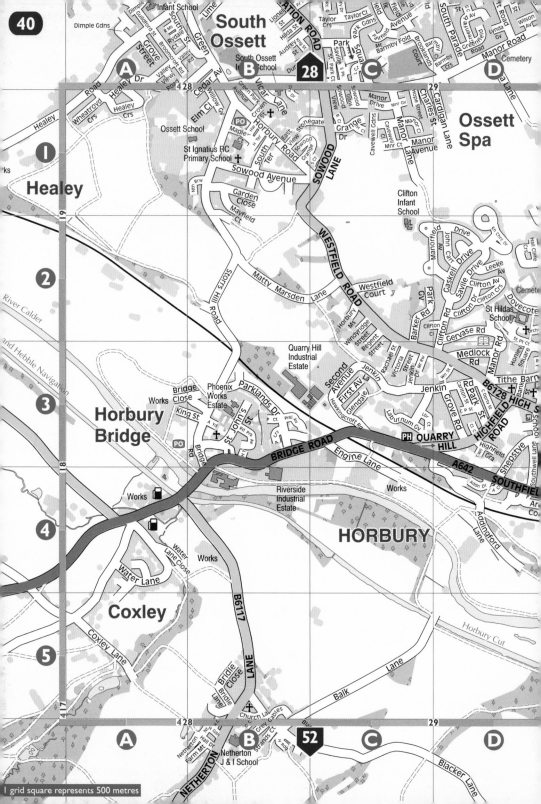

grid square represents 500 metres

E   F   **33**   G   H

Cow

Lane

Southfield Road

Beechfield Dr

Summer Lane

Oaks

Greenwood

Green's Crs

Sharlston Primary School

Woodside Cres

Weeland Dri

WEELAND ROAD

Sharlston Common

Eastville

Northfield Road

Jubilee Rd

Coronat'n

Clifton Rd

Francis Rd

Weelands Avenue

Wood Street

Woodside Av

I

Surgery

Springvale Cl

The Heathers

Hthr Vw

Hthr Cft

A645   WEELAND ROAD

Close

B6378   PONTEFRACT ROAD

PO

Church Close

Birkwood Avenue

West

Crime

Sharlston

Lane

Lane

The Back

Lane

Green

2

Birkwood Farm

Lidget Lane

DONCASTER ROAD

Hall Park Av

Parkway

A638

West Lane

3

Ashdene Avenue

shdene

Ashdene Garth

Ashdene Drive

Churchway

Ashdene Crescent

Harrison Road

Rose Garth

Sandown Av

Crayford Drive

Fernlea Cl

Slack Lane

Dovedale Close

Springhill Dr

Springhill

Sch Cl

Richmond Court

Springhill Mount

Wentworth Dri

Towers

La

46

Works

Lane

Windmill Hill

Foulby

4

PO

N Crofton High School

Crofton Health Centre

Smithy Cl

Crofton Infant School

Junior School

Towers Cl

Harepk Vw

High Street

Walton View

Hare Pk La

Meadowfields Dr

Bedford Cl

Hare Park

Lunx

Med Cl

Priory RdG

Lovell

White Ct

VW

Scott Dr

Priory Rise

Oakdene Drive

Glennie WY

PO

Manor Dr

Oak Street

Ash St

Elm St

Spring La

Grn

Greenside Pk

Greenside Court

Greenside Pk

Manorfields Av

Manorfields

Fourth Av

Middle Lane

Middle Lane

Beech Avenue

New Crofton

Langley Lane

E   F   **57**   G   H

46

WEELAND ROAD A645

Gin L

A 4 40 **B** **34** Huntwick **C** 41 Lane **D**

1

Huntwick Grange Farm

Green

9

Lane

2

Lidget

Lane

3

45

18

Foulby

4

PO

Wakefield Independent School

Nostell Park

Upper Lake

A638

Nostell Priory (NT)

†

Engine Lane

5

417

DONCASTER

Wragby

ROAD

Chapel Cl

A 4 40 **B** **58** **C** Wakefield Independent Junior School **D**

Brickworks

Lane

Long Row

1 grid square represents 500 metres

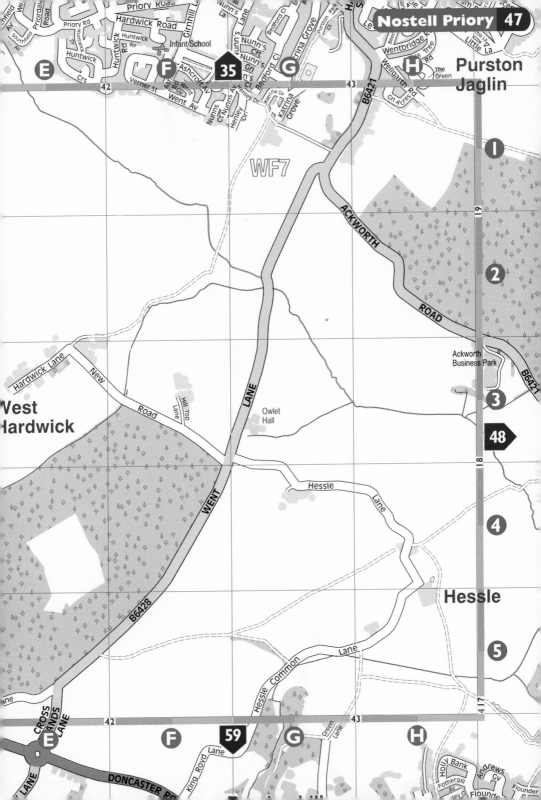

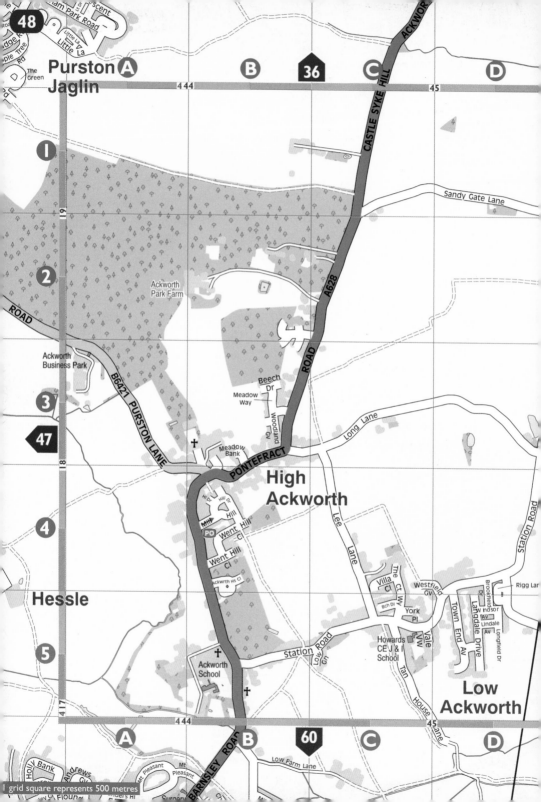

Moor

A639

E　F　**37**　G　H

46　47

HARDWICK

Hardwick Road

Moor Lane

I

19

Water Lane

Lane

2

undhill

ROAD

✝

Darrington　Road

East Hardwick

3

50

18

WHITEGATE HILL A639

4

Whitegate Lane

Ackworth
Grange

5

417

Lane

Rigg Lane

Burnhill
House

Ackworth L

46　47

A639

Tan House Dike

Works

Works

E   F   **39**   G   H

50   51

Stapleton Park Farm

I

New Road

Stapleton
Park

2

North Yorkshire County
Wakefield

3

4

Lane

Leys   Lane

5

River Went

50   51

West Edge Road   E   F   **63**   G   H

West Edge   Road

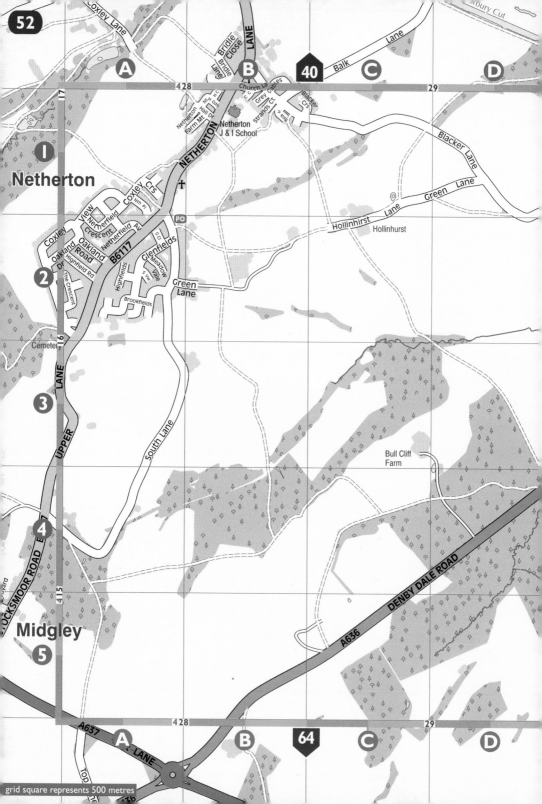

Coxley Lane

Bridle Close

Bridle Lane

LANE

Balk Lane

40

C

D

A

B

Blacker Crs

Church La

Grey Gables

Strands Ct

Netherton Farm Mr

Hall Dr

Netherton J & I School

Blacker Lane

I

Netherton

NETHERTON

Coxley Crs

Nth Pl

+

Green Lane

Hollinhirst Lane

Hollinhurst

PO

Coxley View

Netherfield Crescent

Oakland Road

Netherfield Av

Oakland Dr

Highfield Rd

B6117

Glenfields

Meadow Vale

S Vw

Green Lane

2

Coxley

The Crescent

Highfields

Brookfields

Cemetery

UPPER LANE

3

South Lane

Bull Cliff Farm

4

LOCKSMOOR ROAD E

415

Midgley

5

DENBY DALE ROAD

A636

A637

LANE

A

B

64

C

D

Top

428

29

E **F** **41** **G** **H**

30 31

Works

Broad Cut

Denby
The
Cl
Denby
Kingfisher
Close

Badger Cl

Orchard

I **Cri**

Durkar
Fields

Howard Crs

Asfield Gr

DALE ROAD

PO

Denby Dale Rd West

Primrose La

Milton

Winden
Close

Hollin

Grove
Pk

Grove
Park

Rockwood
Crs

Grove

Kirkdale Dr

Howard Crescent

Howard Crs

Durkar Cr

Barkers
Rd

St James Wy

Durkar
Lane

Durkar
Rise

Calder Grove

DENBY

A636

Hollin
Drive

Howard
Lane

Gillon Crs

Julie
Crs

Av
Colben

Roof

St James CE
J&I School

Blacker

Cliff Drive

Cliff
Lane

Oak Hall
Park

Cliff
Grovel

Cliff

Cliff
Road

Cliff
Road

Dennington
Lane

Branch Road

Bretton
Lane

Woolley Low Moor Lane

M1

Hollin
Lane

High
Lane

Calder
VW

High
Street

Industrial
Estate

Haverold
Way

Church VW

Honds

Moor VW

Moor Vw
Drive

2

PO

Woodmoor Rise

Hopewell Wy

M H Cl

Woodmoor Dr

Wdm
Cl

Aberfield
Dr

New Hall
Cl

Manor Farm Rd

Haverold

3

Mackie
Hill Junior &
Infant School

Painthorpe House
Golf & Country Club

Golf Course

Garden
Terrace

Daw Green
Av

Daw
Lane

**Great
Cliff**

Painthorpe

54
Sports
Club

agiestone

Painthorpe Lane

Jubilee S

Cros
Rd

Baileys
Wk

Hgh Kp Flc

Hollingthorpe
Grove

Av

Hollingthorpe
Lane

Hollingthorpe

Hollingthorpe

Hollingthorpe Road

4

Copeworth
Drive

Russell Av

Edgemoor
Cl

Stor

Moorland
Dr View

Woolley

Woodland

5

Woolley
Lane

Bolton
Wife
Hill

Hollingthorpe

Daw
Lane

Dane Royd Junior &
Infant School

M1

E **F** **65** **G** Low Moor **H** Lane

30 31

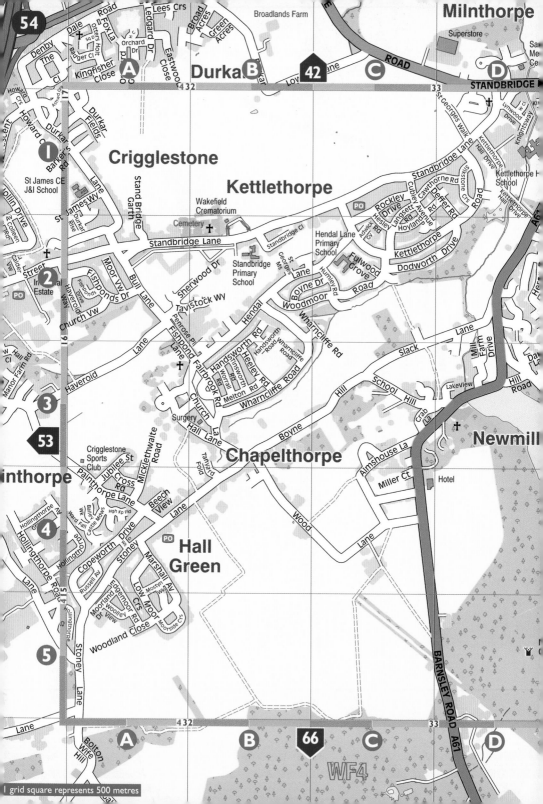

56

Beech Cft

Elmwood Cl
Elmwood Drive

Thornhill Cft
Orchard Cft

Brooklands Rd
Brooklands Av

C T D

Cherry Tree Crs

Cherry Tree Road

44

Thorntree Hill

A **B** **C** **D**

436 37

Walton Grove Infant School

Waterton Cft

Oaklands Cft

Spur Grove

High Meadow

Grove

The

Kendal Rise

Walton

Waterton Park Golf Club

Brockswood Ct

Overtown

I

Langdale Mount

Balk

Sike Lane

Trans Pennine Trail

Golf Course

Hotel

2

16

3

55

Trans Pennine Trail

Briery Hall Farm

4

415

Haw Park

5

Haw Park Lane

Cold Hiendley Reservoir

Haw

A **B** **C** **D**

436 37

68

Cold Hien...

Ryhill Pits Lane

grid square represents 500 metres

E F **45** **New** G H
Crofton

38 39 17

I

Middle
Lane Middle Lane
Fourth
Beech
Avenue
PK

Santingley Lane

2

16

Santingley Grange

Anglers
Country
Park

Wintersett

Wintersett Lane

Lane

Back Lane

Moorhouse Lane

3

Long Lane

Swine Lane

58

Lane

4

415

Dam Lane

tersett
ervoir

Ferry Top Lane

5

Upper
Hall
Place

Lakeside
Estate

Nostell

Common Ing Lane

Brunswick

Newstead

Highfields

Ryecroft Av
Greenacre Wk

Horncastle
View

St George
Cou

Lodges
Cl

Kings

Churchfields

George St

Madeley
Place

Church
View Cl

PO

St Geor

Ryhill J&I
School

School Lane

Cemetery

Cemetery 39

Havercro H
Ryhill

St James
Court

Meadow
Place

Crescent
Road

LANE

East Street

E F **69** G

38

Road
Charles
Chapel St
Laithands La

Park

Hammerton Farm

St
Wood

Mulberry
Place

Mulbe

PO

COW B6428

Regin

W

Station

E 42 F 47 G H 43 17

Cross Hands Lane

Hessle Common Lane

Green Lane

DONCASTER ROAD

A638

King Royd Lane

Brackenhill

Bracken Hl

Garden St

Green Lane

Holly Bank

Fothergill Av

Hardaker's Lane

Hadowsley Cl

Flounders Hl

Flounders

Woodleigh Crs

Andrew

HollyBank

White Moss Cl

Woodhall Dr

Moor Top Av

Bell Lane

Bell Primary School

Hardakers

WAKEFIELD

Francis St

Sykes La

Victoria St

Leigh St

West View

Banks Cl

Heaton St

Banks

PO

Industrial Estate

ROAD

Rhyddings Av

Rhyddings Drive

Dicky

ACKWORTH MOOR TOP

Works

I

2

3

60

Priory Business Park

Terrace

Rose Lane

Wentworth

…lliam School

Athletic Club

…lliam Station

…am

4

415

Mill Road

Hoyle Mill Road

Hoyle Mill

Kinsley Common

Hoyle Mill Dam

5

Morris Cl

…arrgate

Fieldside Rd

Milton Dr

Redland Crs

Ashmount Ind Park

Mill Road

Kg St

New St

Hoyle

E F 71 G H 43

Fitzwilliam St

…tton Street

…nsley Crs

Tomsage Rd

Vale Rd

Park

King …

PO

Kinsley Industrial Estate

Pontefract

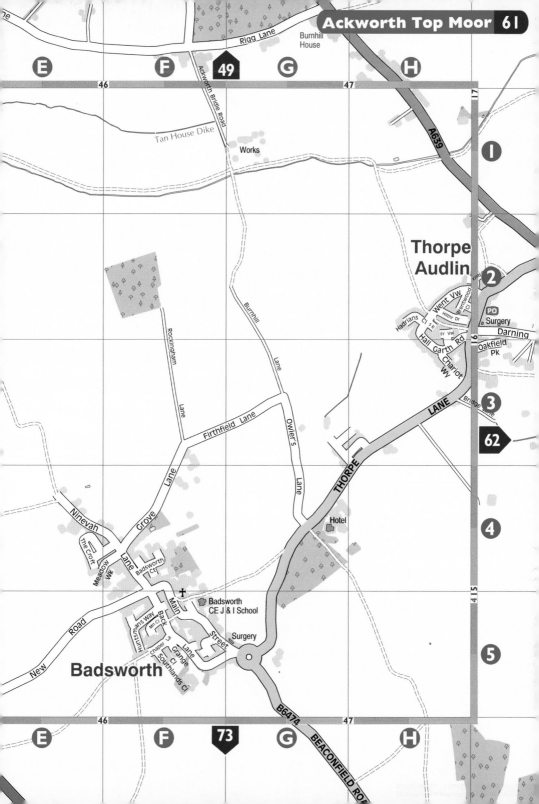

62

Wentbridge

PO

River Went

A   B   **50**   C   D

448   49

WENT EDGE ROAD B647

WENTBRIDGE B6474

A1(T)

A639

1

Thorpe Audlin

2

Went Vw

Brentwood

PO
Surgery

Hilthr Dr

DONCASTER ROAD

Darning   Lane

Garth La

Oakfield Pk

Peartree Field Lane

Watchit Hole Lane

Causeway

Garth Lane

Thorpe Manor

Fr Vw

Hall Garth Rd

Chariot Wy

3

Bridge Lane

LAN

61

Common Lane

A639

4

415

5

Walton Wood House

448   49

A   B   **74**   C   D

Green

I grid square represents 500 metres

River Went

E   F   **51**   G   H

50   51   17

West Edge Road

West Edge Road

1

Kirk Smeaton

2

Middlefield Lane

16

3

Middle Field

Long Lane

Coal Pit Lane

4

ROAD

Harewood La

A1(T)

Crab Tree Lane

4.15

5

Barnsdale Bar Service Area

E   50   F   **75**   G   51   H

A639

DONCASTER

North Yorkshire County

Doncaster

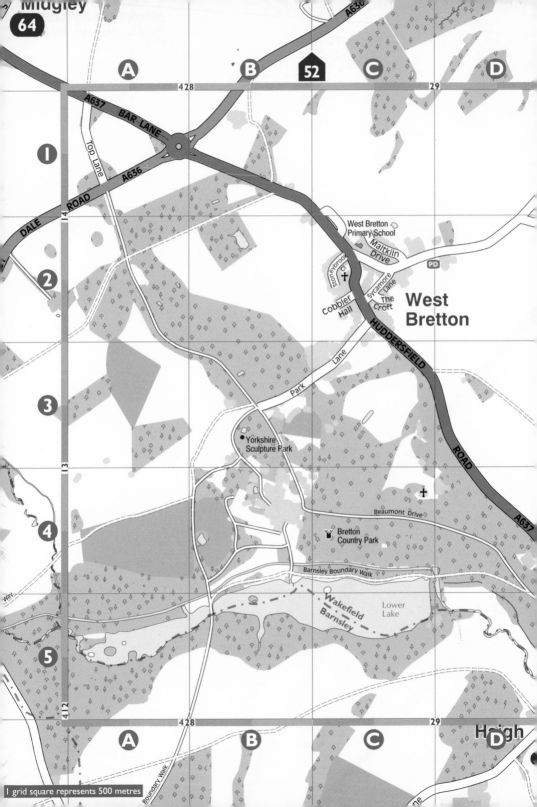

Midgley

64

A B 52 C D

A637 BAR LANE
Top Lane
DALE ROAD A636

I

2

West Bretton Primary School
Maltkiln Drive
Stoneybrook Cl
Cobbler Hall
HUDDERSFIELD
Sycamore Lane
The Croft
PO

West Bretton

3

Park Lane

Yorkshire Sculpture Park

4

Beaumont Drive
Bretton Country Park
ROAD
A637

Barnsley Boundary Walk

5

Wakefield
Barnsley
Lower Lake

A B C Haigh D

I grid square represents 500 metres

A **B** 54 **C** **D**

Woodland Cl

BARNSLEY ROAD A61

432

33

Stoney Lane

Lane

Lane

Bolton Wife Hill

WF4

I

Woolley Moor

14

Gallows Lane

Seckar Lane

Common Lane

2

Water Lane

Lane

Parson

Woolley Pk Gdns

3

Backhouse Lane

The Green

Woolley Hall College

65

Finkle Street

Wentworth cl

High St

The Paddock

Molly Hurst Lane

Church St

Old Mount Farm

Abbot La

Woolley

Lane

Field Lane

Back Lane

New Road

4

Midd

Woodcote Farm

Gipsy Lane

Hawtop Lane

Abbot Lane

5

Woolley

Haw Top

412

432

33

Edge Lane

A **B** **C** **D**

Woodhouse Lane

Warren Lane

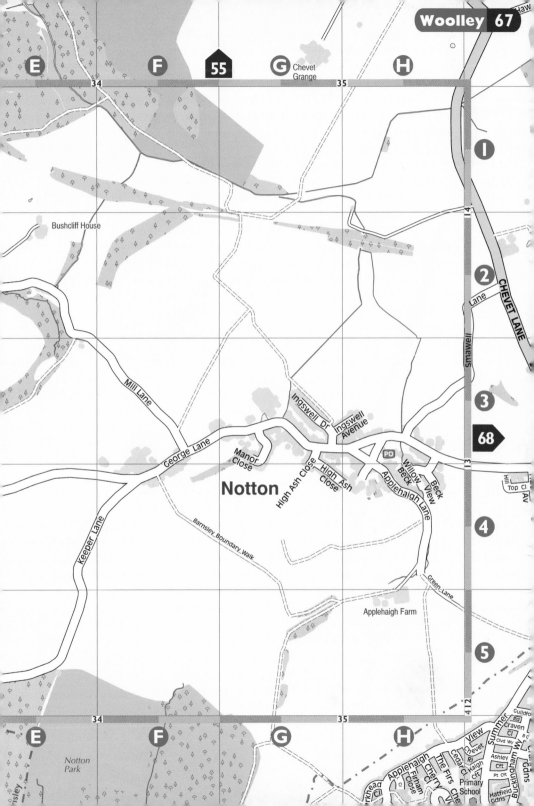

E
F
55
G Chevet Grange
H

I

2

CHEVET LANE

Bushcliff House

Smawell Lane

3

68

Mill Lane

Ingswell Dr

Ingswell Avenue

George Lane

Manor Close

PO

Willow View

Beck

Applehaigh Lane

Hill Top Cl

Av

Notton

High Ash Close

High Ash Close

4

Keeper Lane

Barnsley Boundary Walk

Green Lane

5

Applehaigh Farm

412

E
F
G
H

34

35

Notton Park

Summer View

Chevet

Guildfo

Craven Cl

Applehaigh Cl

Firham Close

Cherry

The Firs Cedar Cl

Buckingham Wy

Ashley Cft

Cl Wy

Haigh Cft

Pt Cft

Chevet Primary School

Hatfield Gdns

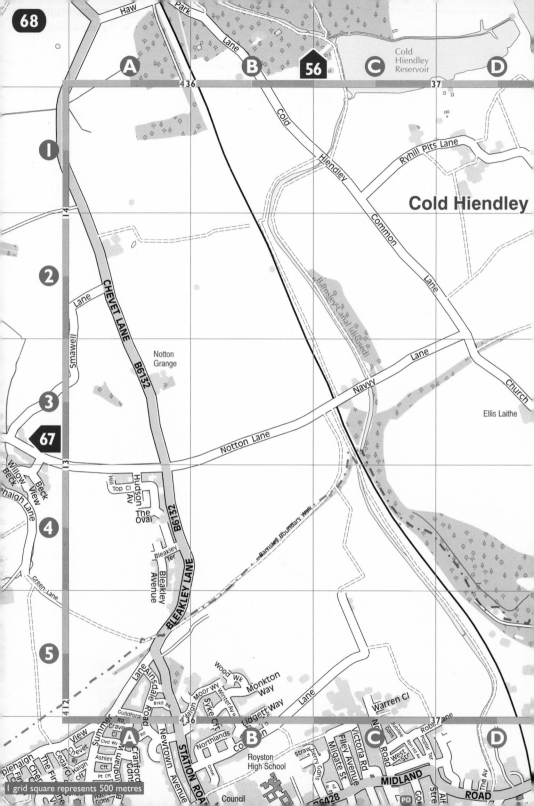

68

A   B   **56**   C   Cold Hiendley Reservoir   D

436   37

1

14   Ryhill Pits Lane

Cold   **Cold Hiendley**

Hiendley

2   Lane

Smawell   Common

Lane

CHEVET LANE

Notton   Lane

Grange

B6132   Barnsley Canal (disused)

3   Navvy   Lane   Church

67   Ellis Laithe

Willow   Notton Lane

Beck   Beck View

Hill   Hudson   Barnsley Boundary Walk

Top Cl   Av   B6132

raghaigh Lane   The

Oval

4   BLEAKLEY LANE

Bleakley

Ter

Green Lane   Bleakley

Avenue

412

5   Barnsley Boundary Walk

Lane   Wood Wk   Monkton

Ainsdale Road   Way

436   37   Lane

Brkd   Haigh Moor Wy   Winter Av   Lidgett Way   Warren Cl   Robb Lane

Guildford   Summer   Syke Cft

View   Crave   Rd   Northlands   Co   Victoria Rd   Filey Avenue   Milgate St

Newtown Avenue   Strawberry Gdns

A   Ashley   B   Royston   C   D

Chev   Cft   High School   MIDLAND

Clvd Wy   Crantford Gdns   STATION ROAD   ROAD

Council

1 grid square represents 500 metres

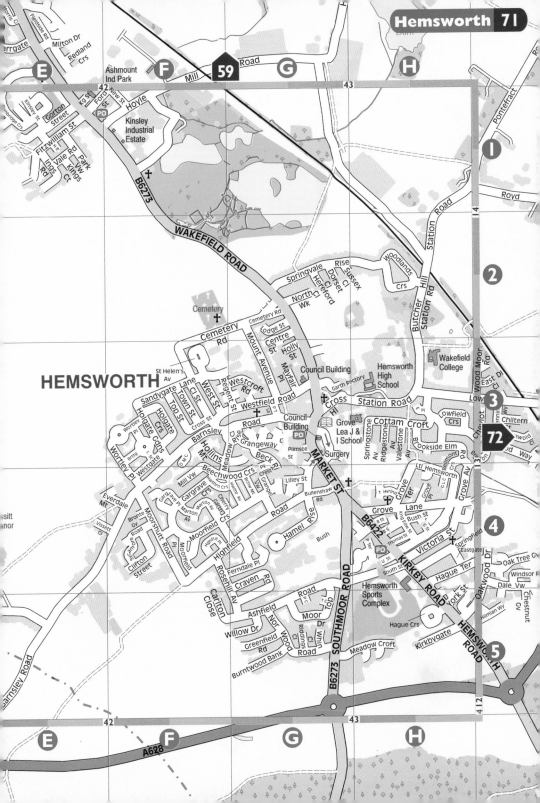

72

A Road

B

60

C

D

1

Pontefract

444

A628

45

Royd Moor Lane

Royd Moor Lane

Station Road

Royd Moor Lane

Elm Farm

2

Butcher Hill

Station Rd

414

Royd Moor

Wood Moor Rd

Wakefield College

East Dr

Hemsworth RUFC

Lowfield Road

3

Lowfield Crs

Cheviot Cl

Pennine Ct

Chiltern Ct

Lowfield Road

71

croft

Brookside

Cotswold

Ringwood Way

Mdw Morvern

A713

Grove Av

Ltl Hemsworth

Belmont Crs

Grove

4

Victoria

Springfield Av

Eastgate

Hague Ter

Oakwood Dr

Oak Tree Gv

A628

KIRKBY ROAD

York St

Windsor Rd

Dale Vw

Hillman Wy

Chestnut Gv

5

Kirkbygate

HEMSWORTH ROAD

412

444

45

A Water Lane

B

76

C

D

HEMSW

grid square represents 500 metres

Badsworth

E   F   **61**   G   H

I

Surgery

46   B6474   47

BEACONFIELD ROAD

Upton
Beacon

A638   DONCASTER ROAD

Tower Av
Beacon Dr
Badsworth VW

2
Upton
ARLFC

Quarry La

Elmsall
Lodge Farm

Avenue
Rose
Rose Cl
Rose Gv
Sunny Av
West Av
East Av
Common
Lane
Crosvenor
Penarth Av
Victoria Ct
Waulkmill
New La
Crs
Bluebell
Thistle Dr
Clover
Wk
Orchid
Orchid Crest

FIELD LANE
Pennine W
Third Av
Second Av
First Av
Richmond Rd
Beech Rd
Little La
Wago
B6474

3
High St
PO
ville Gdns

74

F9

DONCASTER ROAD

BACK LANE

Minsthorpe La

Hall La
4

Minsthorpe

Newburn Dr
Sandfor
Barton Wy
Anston Dr

MINSTHORPE LANE
B6474

5
Stadium Way

MILL LANE

46   Minsthorpe 47
Community
College

E   F   **77**   G   H

Minsthorpe Lane

Pendennis
Denholme
Meadow

South Elmsall

Bailey Crs
Lincoln
Crs

Barnsdale Bar Service Area

E F 63 G H

A639

DONCASTER

North Yorkshire County
Doncaster

I

Long Lane

Warren House Farm

ROAD

WOODSFIELD ROAD

2

Lings Lane

A1(t)

Wrangbrook Lane

Wrangbrook

3

Hill

Lane

Sleep Hill Lane

Hollins Farm

Lane

4

Bannister

Lane

A1(t)

Skelbrooke

5

E F 79 G H

Straight Lane

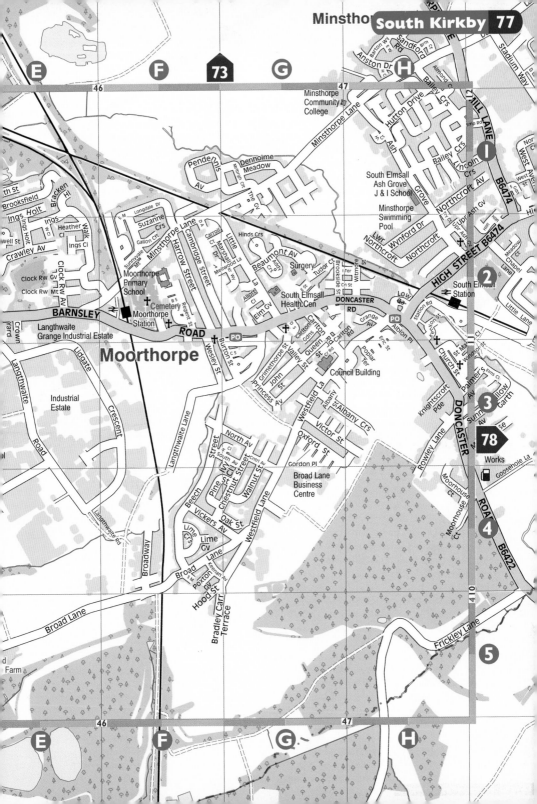

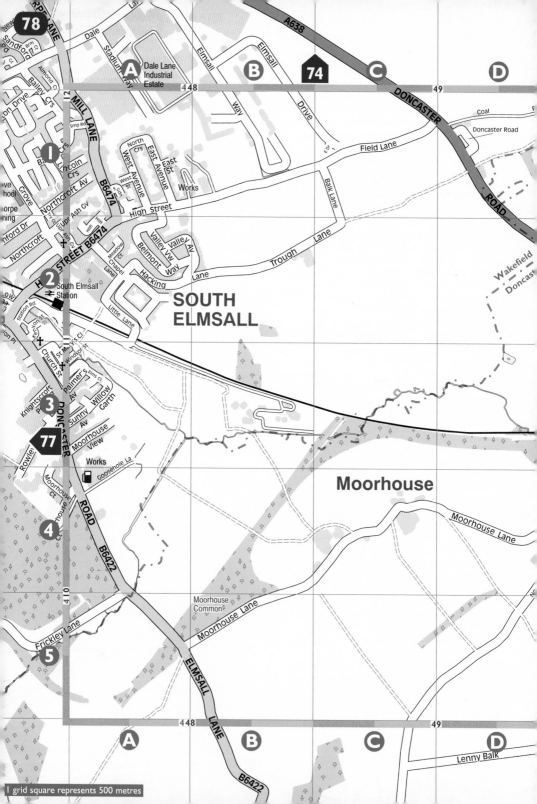